A Cracked Prism

Lorna Catriona Lloyd grew up in rural Essex and moved to Garndiffaith, a small village in south Wales, in 1983 (where she still lives with her two sons). She trained in fine art, illustration and graphic design. Her career includes work as a community artist, teaching at UWCN and running her own design and copywriting business. She is currently setting up a traditional printing studio and writing and painting full time.

A Cracked Prism

Lorna Lloyd

Parthian
The Old Surgery
Napier Street
Cardigan
SA43 1ED

www.parthianbooks.co.uk

First published in 2005
© Lorna Lloyd 2005
All Rights Reserved

ISBN 1-902638-71-9
ISBN 9 781902 638713

Editor: Richard Gwyn
Cover design by Kate Williams / Artwork by Lorna Lloyd
Printed and bound by Dinefwr Press, Llandybïe, Wales

Typeset by type@lloydrobson.com

Published with the financial support of the Welsh
Books Council

British Library Cataloguing in Publication Data

A cataloguing record for this book is available from the
British Library

Acknowledgements

Some of these poems (or versions of them) have appeared in the following magazines: *Poetry Wales*, *New Welsh Review*, *Planet*, *Iron*, *Red Poets*, *Poetry Digest*, *Krax* and *Sampler*. Others have been published in the Parthian anthology *The Pterodactyl's Wing: Welsh World Poetry* and broadcast on BBC Radio Wales. In 1995, *Puddles* won Poetry Digest's international Love Poetry competition.

The author wishes to express her thanks to the Arts Council of Wales, whose award of a bursary helped her to complete this, her first collection.

Contents

For Tom and Christopher

Bluebell Wood

When dusk came to suck
the bluebells grey
I pulled up my hem –
made a hammock
and rocked home
with a bellyful of blooms

I poured her gift
across the kitchen table
but each head had become
a flared nostril
bubbling syrup
like a scalded child's

Her bright cameo lit
the darkening window
as she arranged creaking
stems in sterile jars

Far away, black roots
embraced many-headed
neon ghosts, touched and
held rigid in moonlight

Calendula

I harvested seed last autumn
wintered them in darkness
in spring tiny fossils grew lime flesh
by June embryos became shaking hydra

Seed draws inward like clawed fists
you hid secrets that way – I had to guess
what treasures you held – the knot of a
crushed spider, a GI Joe gun, nothing...

The garden shrieks cadmium orange
sparse petals lash upholstered eyes
like the sunrays you drew – an infant
piercing heaven with blazing spears

Today is your birthday I grew a man
you strum soft notes on a new guitar
they follow my steps along the border
as I snip heads and rattle my bag

You keep time while I unpick
folded minutes from imploded clocks
each seed leaves an imprint in the husk
like a dent on a cold pillow

Granny's Glass Eye

When I spoke to Granny
her one eye never listened;
half her face looked over my head
throughout the conversation.

Sucking a gobstopper once I choked;
spitting it free from my purple face
I knew it would be her glass eye.
Playing marbles I cried,
because the big one I aimed at
looked back at me.
A terrible gnawing wish
defeated any clear thought
to ask her to take it out
so I could stare into the hole it left behind.
I stood by her bedside,
waiting for her to wake,
wanting to open the white pot where it slept
and offer to push it gently in.

That unmoving eye was my only interest.
My eyes would fix upon its mystery
so I never listened to a word she said.
I had this nightmare of losing one of mine –
screaming in the blind night,
"Is my eye still there?"
It couldn't wink or follow,
echo love or dream. It was a fish-eye,
a dead eye of melted milk bottles.

I liked to play 'Granny' – a ping-pong ball,
with a biro iris, floated in a margarine tub
on my bedside table.
They said Glaucoma took it.
Did he take a spoon and fish it out?
Did he suck it hard until it popped?
Did he swallow it?

I don't remember much about Granny but her glass eye
I wish she had left it to me in its white pot
so I could take it out, hold it in my palm
and make it look in my direction.

Free Range Pigs

The boys pretended to gag
at the sickly stench wafting
from a field of free range pigs

A low electrified fence ran along
the border of a hiccupping ditch

Neat rows of corrugated huts
stretched far into the distance
like a refugee camp for freed
internees of factory farming

All wide as mother's sideboard
snouts fat as a child's leg
wearing socks of bristled flesh
yellow lashed eyes searching
in the shadow of mud flap ears

I recalled Grandfather's farm
and the story of the little girl who
climbed into the prize sow's pen

All they found were her
stockinged feet still inside
a pair of bright red Wellingtons

Reading my mind – the beasts turned
studied my children
silent but for laboured breathing
and swishing tails, batting bluebottles

They cleared throats, pretended
to scrape for roots in churned muck

The biggest sow squeezed inside her shelter
rolled swollen teats over a stained map
in the corner, a hiker's gnawed finger bone
pointed toward a pile of infant footwear

Family History

When you were a boy
you saw an angel
with black wings

Hung like a cross
outside your grandfather's
bedroom window

Soles bruised
skin wax yellow
feathers dipped
in petrol skin

You ran to tell
your grandmother
who nursed herself upstairs
to feel her husband dead

There were whispers
and you were kept away
from sick relatives

Ravens, crows, blackbirds
made you flinch –
you slept sitting up

Dragonfly

The twister in the sink
turned spoiled milk
as you gave me your gift

An amber pill bottle
obscured a dead dragonfly
torn wings brushing glass

You found the bottle
rolling at your feet on the bus
and admired the prescription

You found the dragonfly
on the pavement
as you walked the lane home

I keep them in my handbag –
the brown bottle
and medicinal insect
cloaked in oily smoke

Its dull body – an abstract stain
a tiny cathedral of wire
observed from a grim outside

Bottled fractures leaking petrol
an incendiary bomblet
threatening rainbows

Too afraid to unscrew
the child-friendly cap
I hold it to the moon

Dennis

LOVE and HATE were the crude Quink tattoos
pricked out laboriously across Den's fingers

Toughest kid in school, a clever desperate Dan
who lived in a pub and came to school drunk –
popular with every kid he liked

Six foot two at fifteen – shoulders wide as a door
always in detention – borstal – then nick

Teachers noted a high IQ but poor attendance
his capacity for extreme acts of violence – and kindness
a flipped coin chose which fist his mood was in

A difficult but loyal friend –
prison matchstick ship built with lump hammer hands
delicate as a birds rib-cage, sailing over a teak effect mantle

A career in bow tie bouncing – smart disco doorman
famous for smashing a man's skull with a fistful of H A T E
proudly cupping a triple word score in the palm of L O V E

Death of a Diver

Brighton sunshine illuminated
photographs above the fireplace
you swam alongside a leopard shark
an untidy shadow fathoms deep

I stood on a beach too long ago
brown skin – bleached hair
you lifting my baby from the sea
a blonde pearl cupped in huge palms

Dubai creek rippling stars
the girl you married – and divorced
all of us torn and reassembled
in your wake

The divers arrived – huge black slabs
of men – whose hugs shrank my tongue
inside a chilled shell of gin and ice

They sipped malt – told dirty jokes
swayed in lead boots and one by one
toppled backwards like a set
of shiny new dominoes

At dusk the tide flooded each frame –
a promenade of bulbs swung on cables
behind thin picture glass
wriggling limbs hung on a thread of bubbles

Cross Words

Her furniture strained to look modern
bathed in an electric fire's cold glow
red bulbs faked warmth as dusty fans
hummed round and round
throwing flickering shadows
behind artificial coals

Flames she wanted to burn in
as cigarette smoke crept away
from his Swarfega scrubbed fingers
impatiently drumming pools coupons
while she sat determined to complete
another cryptic crossword without words

Crabbing at Walberswick

My sons line up along the quay
like seagulls on a cliff shelf
littered by washing up bowls
and newspapers leaking fish guts

Their attention caught by
silver water ribbons
unravelling gently through bladder wrack
they dip their lines through
crab-infested weed

An army knife hoists
squid embossed with fat kisses
butcher confidence slicing
rubber hoop earrings for
filthy mermaids – sucking eyes
from stolen cod heads – picking teeth
with snagged hooks – gathered
in a sloven of feeding below

They haul barnacled bellies
over stepped shingle –
blistered tresses clacking
with cockle shells

Crabs thrown back into cold fish stew
scum boiling on receding waves
mermaids lolling homewards
in a broth of slaughtered eyes

Crabbers drag bloodied trainers
across sands leaking footprints
they leave quayside graffiti –
the last inky signatures of squid

Away to the Lightship

You left me – five years old
waving from the doorway
I watched your headlamps
swing around and guide you away

I lay in your bed –
smelt Brylcreem on your pillow
played with a splinter of light
slicing through fingertips

Slowly – I became aware
of tremulous tugging
along candlewick spines

And at my feet I saw you –
home from the Lightship
but now a shrunken man
with soft pink mouse hands
and a mouthful of grinning teeth

Hauling yourself
towards me on your belly
navigating deep body folds

I screamed into Mothers arms
she took me to search for you
but Daddy you had drowned

Nocturne

They sleep darkly
wound tightly in linen
chrysalis boys – turning

Tomorrow they'll whirl
around the candle
and push silks
further and further
into cracked palms

Their powder smears
fingers, lips, eyes

It burns like lime

One Small Step for Mother

For weeks we swapped
Apollo mission cards
counted ten-to-zero before
leaping from swings

At bedtime I stared
at the growing moon
caught in forked branches
of the broad oaks
before dreaming
of touchdown

Mother settled five children
on the Victorian horse hair
chaise longue

The TV had two knobs
sunken eel-green screen
a walnut surround
and knitted amplifier
but no outdoor aerial

Rigging the lead
over a curtain track
she pushed scissors
in the end and we watched
the moon landing
through blizzards
of crackling interference

During points
of family desperation
Mother stood like Liberty
her arm raised and receiving
what she could
from Houston

Party Tricks

It was spring
I woke motherless
and felt too young

I thought she could only die once
that I would repair myself
like one of her broken cups
carefully glued back together
fractured, but still in service

But no, she dies often –
when the family began
to unravel and needed her
to wind us back in

Again, in town today
when I shopped alone
and watched a middle-aged
woman take her mother's arm
and ease her off the kerb

It goes on – she fades then flames
like trick candles on a birthday cake
from darkness she returns

Medusa's Gallery

I enjoy my power to fossilise –
And how I can lick my own eyes

I curate a gallery of startled stiffs
Where I have watched the petrifying shift

Of hot, fresh, flesh, to cold, still, stone
Smooth marble ribs – once brittle bone

This is my collection of fine statuary
A sexy – but now inert – menagerie

A breakers yard – a body quarry
Where in time – maybe – I'll say sorry...

To erect flint – where a rub can spark
Remembered sex in this, my brave park

I suck rubies from bitten lips and tongues –
Blow giggles into mazes of rigid lungs

Writhing snake hair alarms my brain
A hero nears – they *creep* the same...

Viper's clever fork makes me squirm
As I taste the heat of muscled worm

My first glimpse of his heroic eyes
He stares back and begins to immobilise

Inside his torso – a pumice heart
Slows his blood as he quickly departs

Rigor captured – instead of pride
A look that isn't dignified...

Mica sweat illuminates this growing nest
Of stags alighting in sweaty, leather vests

Keeper's Pond

Sky stretched drum taut
tricks the eye upside down

Sheep sip under the rim –
a buzzard swims up for air

I drop havoc stones into my head
and watch my selves rush away

As water snatches back
its rocking face

Ship in a Bottle

Your heart refused to travel
like a ship in a bottle

You never visited the sea
content to remain
on permanent waves

I receded like the tide
my rib cage exposed
but my wreckage
failed to touch you

I still wonder
how you became
small enough
to claw your way inside
such a narrow
unforgiving aperture

Only Linoleum

Uncle worked as a porter
in the British Museum
a sudden water leak
damaged its linoleum

It was re-laid
throughout our house
smooth forest green
without stiletto scars
or cigarette burns

A musky smell permeated
our council house

It breathed an odour
of Egyptian mummy
petrified olives – canopic cat

It competed with resident aromas
bubbling lard – hot scones
lavender wax

Mother re-arranged furniture
placed artefacts
from dead relatives
on crocheted mats
on the sideboard

But the floor remained
impervious to new odours

Imbued with an
uncompromising history
we could not scratch it
or make it sniff our minor dramas

Gifts from the Lighthouse Keeper

A Cracked Prism

Dad's gift – big as a cartwheel
was wrapped in tarpaulin and
steered carefully down the pathway

Cutting rope knots, he left us to
peel back the dull green lid from
Apollo's cracked eye

A fierce white wink blinded us
then dunked our elastic heads
into a bright pool of bent sky

Aurora borealis crazied the paving
scribbled over the lawn
raced to bruise red bricks
and smear windows opalescent

Sparks electrified our vision
with a rash of floating stars

Burnt newspapers sent cinder words
flurrying across gardens
writing smut on flapping sheets

Scorched skin erupted in bubble blisters
singed hair shrank to a dolly's perm

Locust kids swarmed at our heels as we
rolled the sun down the road that hot afternoon
hurling rainbows into a cloudless sky –
burning everything in our path

Ammonite

Spiral steps unwound in my palm
'*Like lighthouse stairs*' he said
which made me think he worked
inside a monumental shell
each stair tread paved in gold

But age proved his gift a fraud –
not like starfish or sea urchin
their architecture intact
part of what they once had been

This ammonite was a cast –
masquerading as something
priceless – precious

'Fool's gold' – a chance product
of chemical serendipity
a glittering imprint –
an intricate, baroque swirl

Gathering with its kind –
heavier than shells
pooled behind rock

Until you picked it up
slipped it in your pocket
and gave it to me – a deceptive ploy
to win my forming, foolish heart

Lobster Breakfast

The crate leaked sea-juice
as father hauled it into the kitchen
inside blueberry eyes
searched dry ocean

Mother lowered the condemned
into a boiling sea
her prisoners whistled
at an ear clenching pitch

We mouthed '*stop*'
but she mopped her brow
with a fishy pinny
and alchemy continued

Next morning the kitchen
was neat as a chessboard
and the table laid with rows
of Playdough pink lobster –
eyes poached, feelers limp
and mother, floral, fragrant, familiar

Fists cracked each carapace
we sucked hard on sweet flesh
nibbled inside joke pincers

Dying protests distant
as echoing waves in the mouth
of the chuckling cockle shell frog
bobbing plastic eyes
nodding assent amongst
cheering mantelpiece crowds

Jamboree Bag

A paper pod rattling promise
a waxy envelope of feely intrigue
inside – pink shrimps – sherbet
flying saucers – a bad joke
fake push-up lipstick and a rubber
gemstone ring – this – the big dipper
of all disappointments!

Fingers were desperate for a gift
more delicious than mystery
but all I ever got was a poor girls
dowry of one liners – a bendy wedding band
and sugar morsels melting more easily
than the hardened hearts of skinheads

Their duffle bags bursting with a wild
jamboree of sex – Johnnies – ferrets
Bazooka Joes – Desmond Dekker
Ska – Stomp – Tizer – snake-belts
half smoked fag ends – Rizla+
puppet chicken claws with tendon strings –
begged from the butcher

Bags so full of nicked treasure
their arms dropped to the pavement
swift as plumb lines

This was their kind of lucky bag –
the kind a girl like me
couldn't hope to buy

Hoover Bag

Emptying the Hoover bag, a full pouch
of hair, dead skin.
a fine powder of human detritus,
tossed in the bin.

Queer thoughts are sucked into a vacuum and
clog my full brain.
remembering the way I emptied him –
it felt the same.

I took handfuls of his ashes and watched
him drift away.
my abstract act – bizarre performance art,
but now today –

This simple household chore reminds me more
of supposed loss,
than all our posed, smiling photographs
in their false gloss.

A crumpled bag of colourless fragments –
dull memories –
only repression gives them substance, now
I want them freed.

I empty my decomposing heart, where
truth was confined.
I've pretended to grieve, for far too long –
we never rhymed...

The Only Door with a Lock

I bolted the bathroom door
and wouldn't think
in case he heard me

I stood very still
under the light
until the bulb exploded
showering me in dusty ice

But I didn't move
I stuck my fingers up the taps
to stop them weeping

I was shut deep
as a shriveled pip

Hook

How deep he sleeps now, netted in my shawl,
captured upon my hook,
sucking on a dream nipple,
my milky pouting fishbabe.

Heat Wave

A bee worried inside the throat
of a scarlet penstemon
micro weight testing
hollowed arteries

Lasgarn Wood trembled
swimming edges uprooted trees
hung them from the horizon
like a rack of smoking hands

He wheezed through
a ragged comb of teeth
smiled a curling burn
shivered in the furnace

Swifts fell like black sparks
but the valley remained
untouched – unblinking

Inside his greenhouse
magnified and scorched
parched slugs tough as wine gums
hauled fading contrails
over cracked panes

Each gauzy thread
stitched a wounded sky

Godling

He has drawn a fish-scorpion
with cantilevered body
impossibly jointed fins
and an arched stinging tail

It scuttled from the brain lair
of his infant imagination
through his pencil – escaped
across the desert of his page

His fist raced to the bareness
of its back – pinning the horrid hybrid
beneath a pattern of scaly armour

In control he exorcises his demon
crumpling the Bosch mutation
between brave small hands
its tail fitfully flicking
between his fingers
before extinction in a
waste bin of pencilled poisoners

Like a Godling
he re-invents the world
travelling on wire thin lines
they journey – his hideous hoards

I empty his fears –
smooth crumpled creatures
and store them in a museum attic
of treasured nightmares
beneath the eaves
in a dark he cannot reach

Two Things for Christopher

Each step traced the arc of beach
Mirror waves dragging your twin to sea
My eyes reeled you in

I sat in a reef of frayed nets, feathers
Honeycombed wood, hollow crabs
And a small skull begging release
From a mobile coastline

I unravelled it from things not meant
To breathe or drown together
Rinsed it in a rock pool like a china cup

I had another treasure for you –
A pebble with a hole
An eye centuries peered through
A weakness millennia worried at

Its frame surrounded yours
Until you outgrew my gaze
And smiled down at me in my tatty nest
Your shadow welcome as the incoming tide

We guessed the beast that clothed the skull
Your guesses far more magical than mine

It rests on a window ledge now
Still unclassified
Without an identity
It has known many names

The pebble is a pendant – a pendulum
Swinging gently between

The boy and the man

The boy and the man

The boy and the man

Valentino

Nell sleeps with a carrier bag
of jewellery beneath her pillow
precious, sentimental, broken
a ring with a coral-opal missing
odd earrings – necklaces with broken clasps
tarnished brooches and charm upon charm
without a bracelet to hang from

They crunch reassuringly
as she rests her head
in her trembling house next door
to the Chalkwell to Fenchurch Street line

Valentino, her cat, takes a low bow
and scratches quick-step fleas
while the mail train sends Fred n' Ginger
tapping in their frame

Her teeth giggle in their glass
as Nell slinks inside her cinema of dreams
Kohi-Noor glinting from her navel
a withered hand offered to Rudi's red lips
wedding band spins loose as a hoopla
as points noisily change direction

Visiting Lilly

The stench on entering is fierce
she pisses herself in the black vinyl chair
I've never seen her out of it

Sitting with her great lump of an arm
flaccid with age – heavy on the fireguard

Fallen in the hearth some years back
she burnt off half her face
one eye slips down her cheek
and weeps into the corner of her apron
broom bristle hair clipped flat
around a fluid complexion

Huge legs spread wide thighs
revealing a cave of dark odour
support stockings leak pillows
of incarcerated flesh

Always a coal fire and stick drying
an orange glow her only illumination

She bellows as the deaf do
I try to grasp her situation
to remedy – to sympathise
but she'll have none of it

Ammonia grips me in a panic to breathe
I brew tea and ignore it dripping
from the corner of slack lips

She knows what I'm about
knows her odour is offensive
senility won't release her

Family ties obligate fetching of coal
food deliveries – newspapers
cheery hellos and goodbyes

When I'm gone – she thinks of me
as that Lloyd girl – with the two faces

Night-Watchman

for Ernie La Roque

Slept by day – worked by night
through the week – passed the months
years cycled by...

Nights spent smoking Woodbines
in his shed like a listening herring
slugs suppered in silence
in his nocturnal garden
while he practised spoons for the
Pigeon Club's 'Ladies Nite'

Dead-heading by torchlight
pulling sooty weeds –
turning grey worms
rodent eyes caught in his torch beam
moths stroking his ears as though
he were a fallen moon
waiting for dawn to paint colours
into midnight flowers

Pedalling home each dawn
he wore his face against the weather
battered by wind –
screwed tight beneath the sun
skin shrivelled as a pickled walnut

Rheumy blue eyes watering
through summer
the odour of the chemical tip
buzzing his brains as he followed
the estuary into a rush of gull litter

Under the fly-over into a rash
of council houses scattered
over Pitsea's drained marshes
multiplying year on year
like cubic fungi

Past blaspheming walls
to arrange sweet peas
in Mothers milk bottle

Slept by day – worked by night
through the week – passed the months
years cycled by...

On Waking

I fold into you
and we close
rehearsed as bird wings
flightless without the other

Your hair is silver now
I used to wake
against a chin blue
with stubble
your hair so black
that when you slept
your pillow became
a deep well

I slept in the tunnel
you carved for us
we bathed beneath
one sure star

So many dawns
bleached us pale
like white linen
as though we were
already bones

Eel Creek

Waders pierced the creek's umber skin
elvers gathered thick as silver stretch marks
on our mothers' fat bellies

Worms in Stork tubs leaked oily beads
circling like planets – eel rudders thrashed
the shallows – destroying whole galaxies

Monty hoisted an eel – a beserk limb
thick-bodied as his arm – a muscled rope
sawn in two with a junior hacksaw

It quivered – headless

My Tonic

You were atomic
exploding in a million caprices
I picked you up in pieces
puz zle dy oub ack tog e ther
only to find to find your jigsaw
incomple

Dali

You were the artwork
Mr. Mischievous
sitting on pouting lips
applauding your wife's entrances
the most romantic thing
I ever heard

Still Life

Rotting apples in a bowl
skin so similar to the elderly
in their gathered stillness

And as with the old
decay not always apparent
until the body is moved
and draws a stain

Epicentre Dudley

The Afon Llwyd dragged
itself like a wet limb
over smooth stones
and the screech owl had yet
to alight on the holly tree
outside my bedroom window

The moon, as usual, printed the
casement window on the
floorboards – I shut my eyes
on this scene

It was past midnight when the
tremor struck – my head shaken
from the pillow – perfume bottles
rattling across a walking dressing table

The moon momentarily scribbled
edges of the windows shadow –
and waves gulped at the river bank

But the owl instantly nestled back
inside its feathers and the feet of the bed
settled heavily into well-thumbed boards

I listened in darkness to the BBC's
24-Hour News service
"The quakes epicentre in Dudley –
shock waves recorded in Wales"
 Ornaments had fallen from shelves
but thankfully nobody injured

Nothing much to record really
but that my house had journeyed
millimetres during the night
and that I had been undoubtedly moved

Tourist

Flags were limp
as my tongue

language couldn't
sustain sentiment

the cynic screamed –
told me not to kiss

the worn bronze toes
of a saint's effigy

but I wanted to taste bronze
wear him down – further

eventually this saint
will limp with a hoof

Heart of Lead

A heart made from lead containing the remains of a human heart was found in a
stone crevice in a church in Cork, Ireland. It is now an exhibit in the Pitt Rivers
Museum, Oxford.

I watched as the lead case was beaten –
a rough can to preserve love
the doctor cut away your heart
and pushed it inside
this heart-shaped cyst

You remain in everlasting midnight
without the moon or stars to guide you
but you sleep with angels now
they are your journey's guide
and compass home

Blood motionless – blood mirror still
blood becalmed in a vessel where it
lies marooned in silence I designed

From time to time I remove you
from the crevice in the church wall
tip you up – swirl you around
feel your heart's dull thud-thud

I embrace your weight
wrap it in my shawl
rock you in my heart beat
and before I hide you

Garland you with purple vetch
buttercups, jackdaw feathers
bright pebbles – our children's hair

Love swelling like ice
parting lips of stone

Roulette

Smell the windfalls!

This orchard is not sweet –
it's a boozy pub

Heels explode fruity buboes –
the lawns burst pox

Apple trees bare
but for a few liverish apples
hanging on and rotten to the core

A chaos of daddy-long-legs
dragging fuse wire legs

Cavorting around webs
where spiders play roulette
in spinning wheels

Scotland the Brave

Foot tapping time
as he pressed the kid belly
of his bagpipes –
his favoured child

Ebony mouthparts
pouting ivory and silver
slack belly of Black Watch tartan

Chanter hanging over his kilt
like a broken neck

Body swelling with each
measured breath
drones moaning –
one tone sirens
calling blood home

Throat singing
controlled fingering

He gently dismantled
black bones –
lay her in velvet

Tribal plaid
folded tight –
an angel sleeping
in its own wings

Skeen Dhu –
jewelled with a fat Cairngorm
orange as marmalade

Blade across her throat –
the nipped reed

Memento Mori

decaying fruit –
mercurial anatomies
whispered detonations
a grey-green mould
Lilliputian mohair

unfathomable cloak
slow falling over
porcelain

writhe beneath
imploding flesh

peaches ooze
sticky amber tears
weeping icons –
a corrupt grief
edgeless avocados
collapse wrinkled ears
erupting bristle

ulcerated oranges
slack pores ringed
with bruises sucking borders

apple skin – a wrinkled kiss
drawstring purse of tar

ripe banana lips
squeezing dung custard

artists restricted
spectrum
brush dipped in molasses
palette spilling
suppurating
shadows

Chrysalis

I witnessed a morbid genesis
she shed a skin nightdress

Stepped out of her sick, shrivelled twin
and flew through the wardrobe mirror

She left me pinning her remains
to this and other material

Ladybird Swarm

(Essex 1975)

I wore a smocked frock
that soon became spotted
by a swarm of polka beetles

Polished patent clots
flying down – dropping up
falling sideways

Blood balloons
splitting taut skin
as they
exploded skywards

My mouth opened
wide with horror
as I watched myself bleed
in zero gravity

Frida Kahlo's Itch

This itch is getting worse
and the plaster cast smells bad

I have painted every inch I can reach
my bed is a gallery
and I am a masterpiece

a turtle flipped belly-up
a sterile mummy
a broken compass

but describing myself has become boring
as picking at my edges

I miss my monkey and Diego
they said the monkey was missing me
they didn't mention Diego

In my sleep I was running home
to the blue house
opening my chest like swing doors

I smashed the embryo's glass
and planted the ochre child right here
where my belly button must be pooled in sweat
my baby grew through me like a vine

Cicada sound like scratches don't they?

Could you drop one inside my carapace
so that its wings fret
in my confined spaces
and its filthy nails
scrape a route out
through me

Fly Trap

Yawning bruised fruit promises,
she gargles flowerful juices and
teases with her pierced lips,
curled in a kitten snarl.

Black acrobats tiptoe through fish teeth,
slip and tickle down her tacky throat,
moonwalk into an acid green Jacuzzi.

Zipped lips squeeze abdomens
that drip inside a body bag
fitfully zizzing electric distress.

Excitement bubbles as they
drown in sweet belly waves,
trapped inside a swollen purse,
where all sound, all flesh, dissolves.

Sucking on silence she hungers for
the frisson of insect percussion.

Unhinging clamped jaws
her gaping mouth cups
a wisp of torn wing.

Eating Disorder

I slipped a daisy chain
over Persephone's
reluctant head

She sat rocking
and cupping her ears
against the crash
of falling leaves

Only eating buttercups
she tasted yellow –
dribbled gilded syrup

Counting bloodied
daisy tips she whispered –
Love me not – love me not

His moon rose
my sun fell
crossed shadows
scribbled over her skin

As he snatched
the pale white root
of her hand

I left the meadow
erect with frost
trees naked
summer buried

Behind Nylon Nets

Women swig smiles from a bottle
tucked away behind the Royal Albert
and a photo album with the last
dozen pages awaiting a happy event

Behind nylon nets budgies wonder
at the inquisitive bird in the mirror
whose pecking head rings a bell

Behind nylon nets goldfish chase
marigold reflections and watch
small people swim upright
in square aquariums

Behind nylon nets, heavier curtains
pull shut with theatrical aplomb
and sideboard doors open wide as
Billy Graham's 'Hallelujah' arms!

Beetle

A black beetle
polished iridescent
armour plates shocking
with their dark rainbows

Negotiating rough terrain
with a determination
that defies constraint

Admire simplicity
the way light folds
across its back
unaware of God

Paris Taxidermist's Shop

A moose screams sideways in the foyer
Its rigid, lolloping tongue, chasing moss
Between teeth – missing since Piaf lived

Pea green walls sprout horns like
Hooks for enormous coats
A suspicious turtle with linoleum skin
Ushers customers into a hushed zoo-permarket

Rotten floorboards tilt and creak
Threatening to flip over and tip
You onto the bloodied cellar table

Shelves of aged infants totter
Slither and gawp from death's pic n' mix
Sweeping overhead a mallard mobile
Hangs like a target for toddling royalty
In its shadow a cats licks its smile
So real I ask it a question it can't answer

A daft, dab of a mole backstrokes over
Resin bark, pink embryo hands, soft
As brushed nylon, paddling madly
Towards the millennium

Alloy beetles, neat as cars
Are parked alongside venomous queens
Pinned to red velvet like a tray of
Punk brooches – precious under glass

Tied to a hat stand, a baby elephant's
Unravelling trunk sniffs for its mother
Whose head crashes through plaster
In the outsize department
Frantic eyes search east, west
Her headless ghost haunting another continent

All the undead look through the living
In a timeless spell – waiting for a princess
To come and kiss the century old gorilla's
Horrifying lips – alive

Paris Journal '97

Marché aux Puces

Under a corrugated roof, a man with a corrugated brow pedals refuse I refuse to buy. Monsieur has a turned eye and cigar crepe skin and smokes to cure himself. He sunbathes in a deckchair beneath a forty-watt bulb in his cats' piss emporium. A skeletal cat French-knits his ankles. A tortoiseshell with alopecia-shrink-wrapped ribs inflate/deflate – it is a furry, purring accordion. Tailors dummies recline like weighty Venus'. Mould oozes over nipple-blind breasts. A four-foot high flamenco doll dangles maracas from soiled fingertips – dusty lashes clunk a wink – an infant whore. Her eyes are bluer than cobalt sky inside an Eiffel snow dome. A caged lovebird perches above a soiled newspaper cutting, that reads: '*e-myst-r-grande noise.*' A close inspection of a bowl of pot pourri reveals tiny logs of cigarette ash, several blue bottles and a twist of gum.

For sale: ConneXion. Sex Magazine *with* 1000 Annoncances/ Gas Mask – Clock without time/Telefunken Radio – no knobs/ assorted dolls limbs/a pleading palm/an infant foot/shaved head/dusty eyelashes/dolly with a biro swastika on forehead/ half filled Eiffel snow dome/Attrap Souris /revolving Ashtray – Gitane stubs/3 canvas mannequins – heavily soiled/rubber nipples (used)/Les Pionniers Du Rail-boxed puzzle – complete/ clay pipes/biscuit tin of bone buttons & hat pins/assorted cutlery/tray of cigarette cards/mechanical toys/large quilted bedspread – nylon/sixties chandelier – hotel size

I wind a clockwork soldier; his broken neck clicks sideways –
creaking elbows halt mid-air – tin drum un-drummed –
'Marseilles' long seized. But the lovebird still sings a curious
melody – mechanically adjusting a thimble head & watching me
with ball bearing eyes that keep on flying, away, away, from tiny
sockets.

Passages

Pigeons roost with tarts on Georgian balconettes. Iron lace
adorns flat sandstone chests. Plane trees sculpted from cement
and steel splashed with bleach. Nobody has come to solder on
leaves. Upright rows remember fallen men.

Bar de la Poste

Above my head a painting of a permed poodle galloping through
a field of golden wheat – pink tongue flapping like a slice of wet
ham. I watch the out-world through a slippery moiré window.
Seagulls flung into sky and wind-twisted inside out. Flapping
newspapers raining inky accusations upon the backs of passing
beige raincoats.

Roadside

A plump girl chews gum and blows a blue greasy bubble that grows and grows – she inflates – a giant toad throat expands at my side. If I watch long enough, she'll lick her eyes.

The Go Café

A man pays GO – his eyebrow rises every time he makes a move. I keep looking at his eyebrow. I can't stop looking at his eyebrow. His eyebrow has become the game. Go eyebrow – Go eyebrow.

It is raining. Windy. The café windows rattle inside rusting iron frames. A blonde woman falls asleep in a plate of black olives. The rain is a cut, cut glass necklace – faux diamonds running over her downy cheeks – she rains from the inside. Overhead gas heaters steam her gently. She is a hog head cooking in house wine. When they split her open we'll dip bread into her olive sauce.

The Louvre

Outside. Waiting. Crowds. Whipped by an abrasive wind. Grit sanding off make-up. Our eyes catch razor blades. We make a tent inside a coat and hide. Look down to see if we have to follow queuing feet. We are a headless pantomime horse with eight legs.

Art Trail

Looking for triangles – the Louvre entrance an enormously obvious one but I find a patently obvious one too on the end of a passing red stiletto.

Dog Lover

A trembling Chihuahua cocks its head at me with black marble eyes that are too large and too loose for its tiny triangular head (another triangle!) It wears a knit-one-pearl-one waistcoat lined with pink polyester. I ask for directions in Peruvian. The owner jerks it off the pavement as it starts to piss up my ankle. I hear one of its eyes drop out and roll into the gutter. She doesn't notice. She drags her half blind doggie through the streets. The eye lost.

Illegal Parking

A black hand-painted motorbike leans against railings like a dead ant. Helmet dangles from its thorax.

Tuilleries

A clown without make-up offers rice to sparrows. They circle him like dull brown angels. His palm makes me weep.

Notre Dame

Ooh-La-La – a painted lady – your face the colour of a crepe suzette, your hair ornate as a globe artichoke, perfume and lover following you around the corner of Notre Dame Cathedral. You disappear. You linger.

Picasso Museum

Sandstone catacombs reveal Picasso's brain – pitchfork – goat belly – fractured Mademoiselles with fishy eyes – revolving – assorted garden implements. Horns. A fragment of wallpaper pasted behind a seductress. Another seductress – on steroids – running her volume around the perimeter of a hand painted plate. It is too much – too many – too crowded – one Picasso at a time.

Lost and Found in the Picasso Museum

I lost my purse. Someone kindly handed it in but had slipped a Chihuahua eye in amongst the cents and francs. What might this strange currency buy? A smoked guinea pig? The dried paws of a mole? An albino slug? A bundle of tiny ash twigs tied with human hair? A feather ladder? A day ticket to visit the smoking ruins of Mandalay?

I took it to the GO café – slipped it in the middle of a bowl of Greek olives.

Dead Wringers

Washday turned Monday inside out;
our kitchen dripped interior fog.
The antique wringer in black iron filigree,
sat, tight-lipped, aching to roll geriatric grievances.

Omo-scented steam belched from the
shuddering tub, waltzing over chequered lino.
Slippery tongs delivered steaming nappies
into a chipped enamel bucket.

Reluctant jaws were force-fed dripping smalls
air filled pockets plapped flat
by rollers waggling cotton tongues
scolding stubborn stains.

Pegged from boiling bowl in arctic blasts,
shocked clothes ceded heat to
tugging winds in the hurrying daylight
as jostling neighbourhood ghosts
queued by the clothesprop.

They plumped out generous bosoms,
hung well in y-fronts, minced in frillies,
Rumbad in silk shirts, and socked
the winning goal.

Night frosts held them in rigor mortis
a solid line hung with chaotic
moonstrobed spirits, in
comic fractured poses.

We laughed at cardboard people
in the morning greyness, and danced their
freezing forms to stand and bow
in the searing bacon's hiss.

Pitsea

'New Towns' have grown old
And housing estates have begun to
Repeat themselves endlessly
Saplings grown tall – heads full
But failing to soften stark angles

Half men in overalls lie in sump oil
Beneath hand-painted cars
Alleyways gag on headless strays
Dragging black sacks through brick jigsaws
Clichéd abuse dripping from dry graffiti

Bald lawns sport jumper goal posts
Gardens choke on familiar relics –
Rusting pushchairs – sun-bleached trikes
Knackered motorbikes going nowhere

A football kicked at a steel garage door
A toddler screaming in soiled pyjamas
A girl pushing a pram in stilettos
Infants pierced and tattooed with spit

Nude dolly fossils whimpering from
Sucking clay beds as mongrel dogs
Bark incessantly through wire fences
Like refugees gone mad

Pole to Pole

Children – particles
compelling and repelling
between two magnets

Stargazers

A gift of lilies
creamy white pods
fragile as eggs, hung in the air

In a hot house of deceit they
unravelled frilled tongues
and breathed an odour so strong
they sexed the room

Lips on stalks
strained to kiss his passing hands
and smear him
with iodine powder
each stain – indelible as blood

All his past loves
sniggered from the vase

But I kept their slender
stems too long
left them standing
in foul water

Falling mouths
bloomed like rust
on cut glass

At night I moisturised
with plant extracts
and watched my reflection
outgrow the mirror

Every part of me swelling
while those Stargazers
disrobed, unobserved
in the dark

Who is at the Door?

A mournful gale
sorrowed blows
its bitter jewels
under the door
to weep by my fire

In this white night
wind carved ripples
flood drifting paths

Gently embers sink
and warmth fades as
the blizzard gasps
its last wheeze

Afraid of the sharp
crack of an ice fist
shattering silence as
the snowman knocks

Black Dan

Stood in the middle
of the paddock
head hung heavy with
the weight of winter

A dung-coloured brute
with a mane of twigs
and a tail full of shit

Hoofs sunken in muck
rump steaming in the rain
still as the tree trunks
surrounding his solitary
blot of flesh

Mad eyes focused
on small treats
his velvet soft muzzle –
nimble as boxing gloves
searched out apple stumps
and carrot peelings

Chased over ticklish palms
of school kids in a hurry
the soft petting of many
small hands on neglect

Preserving Babies

Pack umbilical in salt
and store for three months
in a dark (but dry) place
hang in a fine wire cage
from a very high branch
(for airflow and to deter rodents)
when shrunk to a resinous rope
remove the love plait
that joined you

The Healer

Carefully dislodges
the bird from his own
hollowed torso

It is free but stays
resting on the man's
open rim

The bird does not want
to leave a man
it has come to love

It sits like an
excavated heart
so fat in its feathers

Its heart beat echoes
through the gallery
whilst the headless man

Hides beneath his Trilby
and prays quietly for all
who tremble and are afraid

Spiderman

You won't hear him scale your wall
he's too clever for that
too perfect a hero
to disturb your sleep

Nor will you feel his velvet hands
smooth and stroke you
as he ties you up in
sticky silk threads

You will never guess the position
he stitched you on his web
or remember the love song
he drummed for hours

Or how all his eyes
searched your face
for pleasure, for pain
as his fangs pierced your breast

Tickling and running over your curves
clinging and wriggling like water
cocooning you so lovingly

And as daybreak performs her shadow play
he will unravel you slowly
comb your hair and
leave you dreaming

Of trussing up Peter Parker
the quiet man next door
hungrily eating him for breakfast

'Matrioshka' – Russian Doll

A scarfed peasant
lacquered black and gold
shawl bright as a salamander
stretching across her gourd belly

Heavily pregnant and giving birth
to herself, again and again until she
delivers the baby babushka at her core

An ugly child that sprang from the forehead
of a disappointed God

A ten pin parade recedes as
vodka clutched in hammer fists
sweetens rotten meat
numbs the long wait for bread and
jollies the Big Mac mile

Beetroot lips bleed a smile
aching with the effort of repetition

She is unscrewed and screwed up from
queuing for the sickening plethora
of her own skins

Venice Lido

Sipping tea on the balcony
watching gulls – or a myopic
fall and rise of paper
ink running in the rocking lagoon

In the early hours the doctor called –
his cape painted with wax
cracking with every move
his beak stuffed with rosemary
he was a voyeur – I was his treatment
half awake I watched him slide back the sheet
reading my body with hooded eyes
I didn't mind – my sweat loved him
for peeling heat away

Pushing his beak into my right eye –
far as it could go – he stayed motionless
peering into darkness – waiting
for pale red lightening to read by

Malaria forced monks to leave
their marshland monastery
it stood empty for centuries
the doctor saw the dumb bell hanging
heard the mosquito's incessant humming

He understood the girl I was
running through neat Poplar woods
 stripping trees of bark so that I
could draw with perspiration –
a sticky, fragrant resin

He witnessed the damage caused
as I puzzled together meandering roads
straight rail tracks, chiselled waterways
how I came to visit places never visited
places I named – I enjoyed their word shapes
on my tongue as they grew into language

Last night my bed was made
from feathers and travel books
his withdrawal created another dumb belle
I lay waiting on the edge like a baby bird
that would never live to hear its peculiar song

Remaining tea formed a fragile skin
in the cups eye – the '*Brilliance of the Sea*'
sailed into harbour – a floating skyscraper
glittering morning light but hauling shadow
across the Doges' Palace

Moving Histories

Unpacking continues long after the move
unwrapping objects from newspapers
capturing recent history – already forgotten
'Shock April Blizzard'
'Cherie's long Labour'

Objects once cherished now unfamiliar
belonging to the other me who wanders
through her old house at midnight
in a grubby nightgown – whispering
in darkness to unhappy babies

Teenagers now – filling beds to borders
forcing deep voices into corners that cradled
silence too long – their insistent beat pulsing
through timber like fierce weather

Rooms uninhabited become acquainted
with new movement – creaks and hinges
Bakelite clicks flashing blue light

I lay awake listening to the house mutter
its past owner in our bedrooms
watching us sleep – her re-arranged
confused geography

Gathering apples from her ancient trees
trimming her vine in the rickety greenhouse
Sychan River rushing her – and us – forwards

Will I become the old lady who lived
alone in the cottage? Shooing children from
hazelnuts trees – listening for infants crying
in their cots before she remembered
they were grown and absent

Burnt logs still hold their fragile form
in the hearth each morning
a sigh could collapse her weightless bones.

The Lasgarn Boys

Raw-boned they skinny-dip,
bomb off the jetty with wishbone arms.

Knuckled vertebrae punch through
clenched spines, hair bursts
fluid as drowned anemones.

The hooded shoreline trembles.
Heads surface, sleek as seals
then slip back, tight as stones.

Goosed by water blisters now
they stutter for towels
still limp from the last swim,
assume flesh, leave, become men.

The Dead Still Swim

Archaeologists dig
for foetus bones
their worthless architecture
nestled beneath the marble ribs
of Venetian giants

A nun's baby whimpers
from a room
with two sepia worlds

Titian's half moon
cradles the Virgin's
viridescent skin

A lace window adrift
with Putto feathers
gliding through
a drowned chandelier
on the way down – to this

Subterranean hall
where an unborn navigates
opposing globes

Pearl limbs – blue lips
blind opal eyes

It passes
swift as a silver fish
I felt it slide
on my skin

Judy Obscured

(Crickhowell Ward)

I don't like this landscape Judy
your hot sweat – your fat
clinging to your nylon nightie
I can see your huge breasts
through a tangerine sunrise
turning in sleep you are
wrecking on the ward edge

Judy are you sleeping through
the turning of sheets each morning?
Your tourettes '*bum bitch, bum bitch*'
Narrative – a song I untangle hair to –
hair sticky with the heat of pain
pain ripe as splitting fruit

A red helicopter falls like a giant heart
dragging its artery and blizzarding its wake
flakes gross as cherub feathers

A needle through my stomach
and I sleep – sleep soundly in snow

Sheets turned in the afternoon
Judy do you hear my linen snowdrift shifts?
Have your guests undressed in your fats?
Is your body still in conversation?

A supervised bath of warm water
lavender oil anointing an exposed lattice of veins
hands luminous as stained glass
Cannula set in a rainbow bruise

You are turned in the evening
a flesh landscape nurses gossip above
left mumbling in the health and safety night-light
in which you inflate to a zeppelin of voices
anchored by a tangled drip
the digital protest of your alarm
demanding my fear

I don't like this landscape Judy
Black Mountains turned white
your deep grunts and midnight abuse
your folds of skin – and absence

I feign sleep as they flick my drip
burning linen – observations
dark streams into morning

Story Time

He paraded shrapnel pitted shins
where metal too deep to retrieve
still pained him
thirty years on

My obedient fingers probed
jagged fragments as they
worked through retreating flesh

Puckered craters were toothless
mouths muttering on and on

Manoeuvring dot-to-dot
around his random tattoo
I drew enemy lines
on an embossed skin map

I shared his trench – but knew
without searching livid scars
how deep his wounds were
how far a mine could blow a man

Striped Soup

Wasp traps sat on a brick ledge
above humming dustbins

Fall guys buzzed the rim
before slipping into a pool
of paddling antennae
they drifted slowly
to rose-tinted deaths

With tongue between
my lips – I poured striped soup
and dared to touch the tips
of swollen abdomens

Smelling of strawberries
my soldiers without arms
buried in a lolly stick cemetery
each cross – sucked to the bone

My chest decorated with
grinning black brooches

Tea with Aunt Nelly

Is not a dainty affair
Fondant Fancies laughable
paper doilies – a waste of trees

Ringing her doorbell
sends a thrill up my arm
stick-on-lead unpeels her face
as she pulls back chains – fusses keys
peers at my midriff
through a caged letterbox

Kissing her full on Avon
Everlasting Rose lips
I sniff cumin in her aerial hair display
she disappears into the 'scullery' –
the word 'kitchen' equates with 'decimal'

I find her in tea towel plumage
humped over bubbling blue fat
carefully catching floating Samosas
hand-made, perfectly golden
but not quite triangular

Open shelves crammed
with bottled concoctions
exquisite copper plate handwriting
Sellotaped on skewiff
Hot Lime Pickle, Chilli Green Tomatoes

Bullying me into her 'best' chair
she pulls back the ring pull
on the first of an afternoon's lager cans
we eat – making plates with hands
she laughs with her mouth open
as I sample *Hot Lime Pickle*
with the tip of a fearful tongue

Ella Fitzgerald crackles 'Good Morning Heartache'
from a Danset, faux-leather suitcase
after four pints she becomes sentimental
holds my hands in her lap as if I were still a child
she tests me on lineage – makes me pray
for my mother, father and her dead daughter
a hand coloured photograph I greet in the hall
each time I enter and leave – forever three
and smeared with greasy rose lip prints

The Matriarch's Bones

If I could only come across her bones
On the pavement or in the park
And turn them in my hands
Wipe away the dirt – polish them
Carry them shoulder high and sing
Happy as a Mexican

Hold, warm, love them
I'd look for fractures
And fashion a necklace from her teeth
I'd hang her skull over the door
so she could welcome offspring
We could kiss her bony forehead
On the way in like we did as children

Elephant skulls interest me
Inside bone lace drapes upward
They bleach in the sun, change colour in the rain
Termites worship in their baroque cathedrals

I envy the grey herds
Discovering strewn relatives
Tenderly turning the matriarch with concrete toes
Trunks probing the holy relic
Sniffing tusk holes for the ghost
I like their lack of words
No words will do for death

I have nothing to emit vibrations
No clothes, jewellery, books
Letters, ashes, headstone
Marble cross or moss-pocked angel

Her face is growing more difficult to conjure
Memories become folklore
I don't trust them
If I didn't write this, dream her
Or have sad siblings
She would die

I need bones, evidence, contact

First in the Queue

'By 2020, 95% of body parts will be replaceable – some of them literally off the shelf' – Roger Dobson

Jars of pale pink jelly line the lab
labelled in medical shorthand
and stored in rows like home-made jam

Each week I visit my heart –
hold it to the light
watch as blood clots
on coral tracery

A new shape described
in the rose glow
cells replicate, engulf and cling
capillaries intertwine
and build a muscled maze

Where an electric pulse
will soon boom its percussion
through pristine chambers

Meanwhile
I strain to keep time
with the weakening
beat in my chest

My fingers tapping air

Mereulius Lacrymans

Dry rot upholsters
timber with an orgy
of flat fish

Fruiting bellies
pressed against
wreckage

Air sucked through
a hairline crack

Mouth filled with spores
I breathe decay

Miscella
coaxing a passage
sweetly perfumed
and quiet
weakening

Soft creeping
lacework
prying – forcing

A gentle
dismemberment
of joists

Asthma Song

Wood pigeons rehearsed the same three notes
over and over in the oak canopy

I joined them as I practised flute on summer
afternoons – fingers plugging – unplugging air

Even when I slipped the instrument inside
its sleeve – low breathy notes lingered

Like my lungs wheeze – an irritating melody
that refused to end

I, the unseen watcher of others' games –
skipping ropes swung invisible – clapping n' chanting

*Two, six, nine, the goose drank wine, the monkey
chewed tobacco on the streetcar line...*

Cart wheeling sisters cutting space with scissor legs
hopscotch pebbles kissed for luck in hot palms

Manic limbs danced over chalky numbers
as I blew through the window – in tune with their beat

*The line broke the monkey got choked and they all
went to heaven in a little row boat – clap clap – clap, clap...*

Weird Webs

Scientists from the Marshall Space Flight Centre have been feeding spiders drugs to test the toxicity of chemicals.

Spiders on marijuana start webs
but never finish them
sometimes they fall off
without a safety line

Spiders on speed weave furiously
but leave huge stringy holes

On caffeine, webs lose shape –
just a few hanging threads

Spiders with habits...

Stare at flies for eight hours
without tension
leave mates uneaten
hang unclean in bloodied silks
meat unwrapped

I saw one descend
from Aunt Nell's ceiling
truss up a stray Nescafe granule
and hoard it like mummified crack
behind her smiling Elvis clock

IVF

A fluid code of time
spiralled back genetically
to the big bang ejaculation in a sterilised jar
a milky soup of minutiae – encyclopaedic volumes
links explode offering millions of variants; we pray for one
unravelling chains rescued by a glass ark
with clasped hands we listen to piped music
awaiting a nova burst or black hole

An egg planet with satellite sperm
thrusting furiously to unlock our inheritors
astronauts jerk broken umbilicals
hope eliminated by abrupt ends

The alchemist – a technician
no dancing Luna threads from immotile lead
messages beyond numbering – arrested at zero
microscopic love dies on the petrie dish
ancestry ended – gene legacy bankrupt
we cry for the ovum and the sperm
as if they were lovers – unrequited DNA

He smiles a routine smile
kindly ushered to the door
we pass another couple cradling
a warm jar of cinnabar spermatozoa

Home to our semi-detached – a pastel
mausoleum hung with dusty mobiles
a clown grins from a Babygrow
wriggling with a ghost baby
wailing for attention from inside a locked drawer

Wrapped like a bird's egg in cotton wool
a positive blue litmus wand
lullabied in my palm

Future Valentine

Scientists have successfully transferred genes from a luminous jellyfish to plants –
the application will be horticultural. Farmers will be warned of subtle changes in
atmosphere by the glowing response of crops.

Far from the ocean deeps
this plucked rose
hides a fishy tale
a jelly-gene torpedo
thrust through species

Science reduced to novelty
– a gift for you

Breathe on this rose
and it'll light your eyes
with luminescence
you'll smile and remember
buttercup love blooming
under your chin

But if I gave you a jellyfish
you would scream
limp without water
it would trickle frilled stingers
thorough your fingertips

This rose remembers
hanging from a wave
like a melting chandelier

This rose flowers
a borrowed light

Bad Weather

Indisputable negatives turned hills black to white
a filthy, clinical landscape unfolding in a sub-zero furnace

Filipino nurses printed grey feet on the hospital roof
a joyful pirouette of dance manual steps

They threw handfuls of snowflakes into freezer air
mitten slush melting on their hot, pink tongues

Black Mountains swallowed by a glacial dark
shadows cascading and clinging to unstable horizons

Ice intimidating routes through hairline fissures –
primroses perfectly described by a mantle of crystal stars

Sleeping with the body in dispute at my side –
a ranting mute wrapped in a shroud of journal entries

Holding her hand in the moonless space between us
we listened to bad weather – its soft but bitter howl

Air

Circulates – in – out – regardless
of where it enters or leaves

It didn't swell your premature lungs
but dried on the petal of your tongue

It cooled in the holes of your shawl
while live babies screamed down the hall

As nurses tidied you, quietly, away
I held my breath for you, still do, today

Shrine Diary

Rodents that plagued her
turned to violets as she died
a child embraced her foot
his tears washed away soil
from toes that never walked

Dirt crept upon her skin from
too many shamed hands
she sleeps eternally now
by the saffron light
of alabaster windows

A midnight dome of glittering
stars and cyclical moons has
become her skull's cap

She hears the shuffle of tourist feet
and each guides whispered soliloquy –
not the choir of angels she hoped for

But – she admires St. Sebastian's
porcupine breast – the colour of his
ancient heaven-lit blood
his pain – a bitter potion she shared

Her carved bed – a marble lidded
bath where her deformed bones
swim in petrified violet seed
she fingers lace like points of air

I follow a curl of cigar smoke –
and the click of alligator heels
on Veronese marble – my eyes
unflood in low October sun

Wind rips the dirty flag –
tears a candle sconce from stone
a sick bird rotates in a web of feathers
spiders shed pale ghosts at her door

Waiting

Autumn drew up its bridge
leaving me giddy in this tower

I stoop – stammer – dislocate words
blood slows – bleaches hands

Liver spots pinpoint
my body's journey
fingers curl inward in sleep

I try to conjure heat
but friction burns

There are no seasons
I grow thinner each day

Frail bones and grey hair
like something washed ashore
that can't be named

Running a Temperature

As the coach passed King Sedgemoor's Drain
it offered a million cool lips to kiss my neck –
at the back, where the angel gazed.

I stitched a Passionflower in silks.
Christ's little fretwork Catherine Wheel.
Fire and sex spun among black leaves.
My needle busily securing
The Stations of the Cross.

Passing the traveler – a winged visitor
from the west, we journeyed home from Eden.
The route home evangelised with dodgy
voices from the back: "*Come before him
with happy songs!*" I didn't think so.

April sun lit peroxide hair.
I was burning along all edges,
incandescent with radium,
a joyous glow accompanied
the ticking of clocks.

Motorway spine joined watery pages.
Puckered with scars on spilt levels
where wader's pierced waters skin
and wasps ate their journeys home.

Mouths full of stolen 'Miraculous Berries',
even after an hour they're said to
camouflage the bitter taste of quinine,
our taste, far less exotic.

We spoke of the new Magnolia –
'Heaven Scent' – how I'd sleep
eternally in the belly of its roots.
We spoke of reduced circumstances –
canvas swinging across the door.

Black pinheads attached irises –
tiny morphine pupils with a wide-angle lens.
Later, sore eyes closed in a room smelling
of ink, linseed and turpentine.

You interpreted my wracked torso
with a thick red impasto – hot chilli jam.
I was gathered on your palette
like favourite ingredients.

Now I doze above a fridge lullaby.
You'll not recognise your painting
as your mother. It is an arrangement
in red and black by an unpretentious child.

But it is I – fuming in your oils.
You're filled with my disorders.
Painting me through long nights
wintering in hot-housed Oxford.

I wasn't pretty, or buried, or even there.
But with you – always on your palette,
in the spaces between your words,
crowding, overcrowded canvases.

The Oxygen Tent

Floating nurses peered
inside with milky opal eyes

I pushed poker-hot fingers
through x-ray walls
to melt and drag their skin
through pools of smudged stars
swimming like fish in a dry aquarium

The hiss and blow of oxygen
muffled mother's words

Lifting me into focus
her face resumed edges
a sepia fleck floated
in a pale grey iris

She rolled my name on her tongue
Like a twist of barley sugar

Rough laundry hands
Swung the barrel of phlegm
Grown too heavy for frail ribs

Puddles

You know the way a puddle reflects the universe
Inviting you to leap into heaven
That's him
Pretending to be deep
When an inch down I hit rock bottom

You know the way an onion looks
All that golden-varnished skin
That's him
Unpeeling his clothes
Disappointment makes me cry

You know the way a Lighthouse shines
That's him
Illuminating my life when turned on
But then it's two in the morning
Pitch black, and I don't know when, if, he'll be back

You know the way a poem
Sometimes makes an absurd connection
That's him
Lyrically professing his affection
When I know he borrowed every word

Age of Reason

Not the years of muscle and bone
that physical growing time
has gone – and quickly

This is the layering of ideas
their swelling intellects
tough as artichoke scales

Skin, upon skin hardening
spiked with reason

But they allow me
to peel back and peer deep
tenderly stroke silk hearts

They're snug inside
philosophical globes

Young men quilted in
sharp skin – they cradle
a dangerous light

I fight for them
with the quiet violence
of life saving inoculations

Baking Day

Floury hands turned
the television on
its bakelite knob
covered in white dust

The screen warmed
like Mother's oven
as she baked fairy cakes
to encourage my weak appetite

They rose as she sat me
on her lap to watch
Winston Churchill's funeral

My head rested on her bosom –
rising and falling to the aroma
of hot vanilla essence

We followed the cortege –
the sombre hypnotic commentary
her fingers smoothing my brow

I took her hand –
picked sticky dough
from beneath fingernails
rubbed intricate silver tracery
from many cracks
in her dry skin

Played with cake wings
while the screen
punctuated his end
with a receding
white full
stop

Wordless

Her brow rose like dough and conversation shrank
meaningless as print across a burst balloon

In an armchair with a garden view she smiled
at a robin tugging fat through a swinging wire cage

Her intrigue expressed through artful mime
as she gestured for me to watch it feed

Mother, disfigured, without appetite, found humour
in that bird, a fragile friend, a shared hunger

Tegenaria Domestica

She spider –
peeling wet skins
in a closet of frozen smoke
she outgrows her season

Knitting spiderlings
inside dirty papooses
black threads fidget
inside robust gossamer

She fondles pinstripe
bee fur, veined lace

The back porch
hung with
dead men's clothes

Wind never shook
these sagging
corner cabinets

Closeted from
heat and ice
this is her
undisciplined state

As I enter
black lightning
earths to a crack

How monstrous
has this house guest
become?

Carlo Cactus Collector

Imprinted rings on sand trays
marked his desert after thorny gifts
to family and friends
paraffin cans empty
but winter near

Dismantling staging piece by piece
he stacked green panes in newsprint
wiped clean his black book of script
where purchased – date flowered
Latin names he was too shy to speak

Countless times they drew his blood
but he loved them like bitter children

Incongruous petals would unfurl
from armoured stems
to shock with bright stars
those who called them ugly

He admired a flower on a spiked globe
offered it to me with a smile

I carefully removed the bloom
from its swollen belly
pressed it between his handwriting